BEYOND THE
GIFT *of* LIFE

MAKING THE COMMITMENT TO BE A STAY-AT-HOME MOM

NIKKI D. BLAKE

Order this book online at www.trafford.com
or email orders@trafford.com

Most Trafford titles are also available at major online book retailers.

Printed in the United States of America.

ISBN: 978-1-4269-5549-5 (sc)
ISBN: 978-1-4269-5982-0 (hc)

Trafford rev. 02/15/2011

 www.trafford.com
North America & international
toll-free: 1 888 232 4444 (USA & Canada)
phone: 250 383 6864 ♦ fax: 812 355 4082

DEDICATION

First of all, I would like to thank my Lord and Savior, Jesus Christ, Who put this book on my heart about eleven years ago. Without Him, I would still be wandering lost without direction in my life. Next, I would like to thank my husband, Reagan, for all the sacrifices he has made over the years to allow me to be at home with our boys before they were in school and to teach in their school, when salaries other places would have made more sense financially. I can never repay you for the gift you have given me. Next, I would like to thank our boys, Colt and Cade, for giving me more joy than I ever believed possible and teaching me, by example, how to love and be loved unconditionally. Finally, I could never have written a book such as this without growing up with the consummate example of the stay-at-home mom, my mother, Mary Gill. Many people say of friends and family that they have "always been there," but my mom literally has always been right there for me my entire life. I am so grateful for all the years she has modeled for me what it means to be a good mom. My late father, Bobby, passed away two years before I married, but if he were here today, I hope he would look at his legacy of "family first" and be proud of the choices we have made. Thank you, Daddy, for understanding the heart of my mother and the three mothers you have raised. To Gay and Kristi, my sisters and two amazing mothers themselves, thank you for your commitment to family and for loving me. To God be the glory!

INTRODUCTION

I would be less than honest if I did not admit that being a stay-at-home mom for the last seven years has been the most difficult job I have ever chosen to do, but I also joyfully announce **without hesitation** that it has been the single most rewarding experience of my life. Before becoming a mother, I never dreamed that caring for two small children of my own would be even more challenging than managing the one hundred-plus seventh and eighth graders I was responsible for each year as a teacher in a suburb of Houston, Texas.

I thought my days of feeling under-appreciated and underpaid were finished. WRONG. Little did I know that those days were really just beginning, and on a much more personal level. I also did not realize that I had agreed to a position for which there is no comp time, down time, coffee break, holiday, or vacation. What was I thinking?

Then a life-altering moment took place. My first son was born, and I was forever changed. As I looked into his face for the first time, a sudden awareness of his complete helplessness struck a chord deep within me that I was not even aware existed. In my heart, I vowed on that day to be his protector, teacher, nurturer, healer, and counselor because he needed me desperately, and I fully intended to satisfy his every need to the best of my ability. In doing so, my needs began to be met, as well.

There is no feeling like the love of and for a child to change what is empty to full and what was once an existence of self-centeredness to one of self-improvement and completeness. Being responsible for another human being made me want to be better and do better than I ever had before, but the reality is when you commit to having a child, you only have one chance in his formative years to train him in the way he should go, while molding his sense of self-worth and convincing him that he is loved. There is no rehearsal, and "do overs" are not permitted. We are still destined to fail at times, in small ways, but we must be determined to make right choices in matters of utmost importance. Are you feeling inspired yet?

Because children are our most precious gifts of all, I believe we are called to be good stewards of them. You see, to give your children the gift of life is simply not enough. Each child also fully deserves a commitment of time and attention by his mother **and** father in order to thrive.

During the course of my ten years of teaching and forty-plus years of life, I have had the opportunity to interact on many different levels with both working mothers and the children of working mothers. May I suggest to you that the nagging guilt the working mother experiences each day as she leaves her young child behind and the undeniable feelings of abandonment the child experiences are voices of warning to each that at least one of the laws of nature is out of balance.

The decision to write this book comes from a passionate belief that our first and foremost role as women is to be mothers to our children. Somehow that concept has been diminished with time through our efforts to create equality between the sexes. I do not believe that God ever intended for the sexes to be equal in the sense that both are equally qualified for every job. God has given us different anatomies, different intuitions, and certainly different perspectives on and interpretations of the world we see each day. Each of us has a role to play in maintaining **the most important factor influencing our world--the family**. Fathers can and do make wonderful stay-at-home parents as well, but nature provides that the **mother** be the primary caregiver, if at all possible.

Much of the information presented in this book is not new and is mostly common sense based on what was once common knowledge. I believe it is possible that the young mothers of today are not making informed decisions and need to be reminded of the reasons why so many generations of mothers before them have made commitments to stay home with their young children. The reason why many of them do not choose to follow their predecessors is not simply that today's women have more opportunities than those of forty years ago, but rather that they have come to revere this variety of occupational opportunities as somehow having liberated them from the humdrum lives the stay-at-home mothers of the past were powerless to change.

My hope is that this book will help rekindle the **true** spirit of motherhood and place a new emphasis on the importance of a mother's role in raising her children while also raising our awareness of how wonderfully fulfilling that experience can be. If I can convince one mother to make this choice or one reluctant husband to allow his wife, or even himself, to be the stay-at-home parent, then my efforts in writing this book will have truly been worthwhile.

For those of you who have already made this commitment, I hope you find it rewarding to read some encouraging words that not only validate what you do, but also serve as a reminder of why you made this decision in the first place, (especially on those days when life at home is particularly unrewarding and unfulfilling). No, your worst day at home with your kids will not be better than your best day in the workplace, but the return on your investment of five or more years will pay off long before your child reaches maturity. Just as the interest on any investment rolls in periodically, you will experience small rewards as you watch your children grow, learn, and develop into happy, secure, well-adjusted individuals. In addition, you will experience the gratification of knowing that you made your child a top priority in your life by giving as much of your time and attention as possible. The most rewarding lives are those lived without regrets.

A special note to single moms. . .

If you are among the millions of single moms who have no choice but to work outside the home, my prayers are with you. When circumstances beyond our control call a mother away from her children, everyone is affected negatively. Just as I understand your struggle, I also understand that you are making every sacrifice possible to ensure the welfare of your children. Brava!

The most important *thing* he wants

Is not a *thing* at all.

It is **his** mother's loving arms

To teach him how to crawl,

To catch him should he fall.

Chapter One:
Material vs. Maternal

According to the U.S. Census Bureau, Statistical Abstract of the United States, the percentage of **married** women with children **(where the husbands were present)** who were stay-at-home mothers declined dramatically from an impressive 72.4% in 1960 to only 29.4% in 1998. Furthermore, of that same group of women, the percentage of stay-at-home mothers with children under the age of six fell from a respectable 82% in 1960 to a mere 36.3% in 1998. In 2004, the percentage of married couple families with children under the age of 15 whose mothers stayed at home "to take care of home and family" was an alarming 24%. Fewer than one in four of married mothers is choosing to stay home to raise her children. These statistics clearly beg the question of "Why?" Nevertheless, before examining the effects of these statistics, we must first examine the causes.

During the last few centuries, millions of married women have joined the work force either because of necessity, by choice, or by what seems to have become a forced choice. In some instances, women have been placed in the role of breadwinners of their families because of divorce, death or illness of a spouse, or some other circumstance where the unexpected has led to the need to seek employment.

Like many other girls who grew up in the 70's, I chose to go to college after completing high school to fulfill my dream of living an independent, "Mary Tyler Moore"/career-girl kind of life, while still hoping someday to marry and settle down to raise a family. While we were a little more serious about our college educations than many women of my mother's generation who openly admitted to attending college in order to achieve their "MRS." degrees, we still viewed it as a stepping-stone to a future of career (second) and family (first).

Within the last twenty-five years or so, the choice of whether to prepare for a career or not has all but become obsolete. The present demand for a college diploma for long-term, lucrative employment in this day and time is equal to the demand only a few decades before for a high school diploma.

We American women have found ourselves caught up in a quest for power and equality in a traditionally male-dominated society that has pushed us to a point of frustration unmatched since the days of the women's suffrage movement. Our indomitable spirits tell us that because we now have unlimited opportunities available to us, we can and should **do** all we can and **be** all we can with equal degrees of accuracy, efficiency, and effectiveness. And, if we fail (which we often do), or choose **not** to do it all, our own sisterhood of women will be first in line to remind us of our inadequacies, while the men stand ready to deliver a strong dose of "I told you so." I once heard a young woman during the introduction session of a class I was taking describe herself as someone who works full-time and is a full-time mom. How is that possible?

Just as completing one's education and beginning a career have all but become the rule, staying at home to raise one's children has become the exception. We have been programmed into believing that no longer is it enough just to be a wife and mother, and those who choose to do so are accused of "setting women back." Society dictates that we must also prove ourselves in the working world to be considered a "whole" woman. We have allowed ourselves to be belittled into giving up the one job that will mean the most to the future of our society. Just as a whole is the sum of its parts, does not the character and quality of the individuals determine the character and quality of the community? Pope John Paul II once said, "As the family goes, so goes the nation and so goes the whole world in which we live."

Most would agree that as a society we have little to show in the way of improving the character and moral integrity of our nation (from the offices of some past Presidents of the U.S. on down) in the last four decades. Could it be that we as mothers in our efforts to win the almighty dollar and level the playing field against our male counterparts and in turn strengthen our positions in society have really, in fact, become the weakest links in this social chain?

In an era when teen pregnancy, teen drug abuse, violence among teens, and teen suicide are at an all-time high, should we have to wait until our children join these statistics before asking ourselves what more we could be doing as parents? Never before in the history of our nation has the need for stronger parenting been more crucial, and still we continue to shun that responsibility to satisfy our own needs to feel equal, valued, and successful in the eyes of our peers.

You might be surprised to know that in a survey published in the June/July 2001 issue of *Parenting* magazine, where working and non-working moms were asked to respond to the statement "I think that what I am doing is best for my children," only 70% of working moms agreed with this statement versus 91% of non-working moms. Furthermore, only 67% of working moms responded favorably to the statement "I think that what I'm doing is best for me" versus 77% of non-working moms. Therefore, staying at home with your children not only improves the way you feel about the care they are given, it also improves the way you feel about yourself.

When we as women accept the idea that to sacrifice, love, and nurture is somehow substandard, we really are proving ourselves to be the weaker sex. What other animal on earth ignores its own maternal instincts in such a way? I am challenging you to find that sense of accomplishment in a job well done in the **home,** at least until your children are old enough to start school. Just give them your love and undivided attention until then, the one gift that they will keep and cherish forever and never outgrow.

It's what I say, not what I do.
My words, not acts, I say are true.
I go to work each day for you,
So you can have things others do,
All nice and new.

I do not go to work for me.
I sacrifice for family.
I have to leave you here each day,
I have to work, you get to play,
That's fair, I say.

And when I bring you home the toy,
That fills the dream of ev'ry boy,
Just days from then, it's not enough.
You think that you might need more stuff.
Well, that's just tough.

You don't respect how I have toiled.
I've figured out you must be spoiled.
How dare you cry for me to stay?
I couldn't stay home anyway.
Forgo my pay?

And one fine day when you are grown,
And have some children of your own,
You'll understand the risks I've weighed,
The sacrifices I have made,
And who has paid.

Chapter 2:
The Apple Doesn't Fall Far...

Many people have children and continue to work out of some sense of financial obligation to their children. They believe the more material *things* they can provide, the more loved their children will feel. Parents are always saying, "I want better for my own children than I had growing up." Nevertheless, no matter how noble the idea may sound, each day when the mother chooses to leave her child behind to go to work, the message is clear in the child's mind, "Mom would rather be somewhere else than with me." He may even come to the conclusion that he is not worthy of her attention. One message, however, becomes blatantly obvious to the child, and the lesson is taught (no matter how unintentionally) that <u>money really</u> <u>**is** more important than family.</u>

Without a doubt, the most prominent role models in a child's life are and should be his parents. When any parent is motivated by money and material possessions, it stands to reason that the child will usually follow suit. As he or she observes his or her parents' drive to acquire more *things,* even at the expense of the child, a strange phenomenon occurs. Instead of the child's being grateful and satisfied by all the *things* the parent provides, the exact opposite occurs. He or she begins to believe that *things equal love.* Having been clearly taught that earning and having money are much more important than spending time with family, the child will also grow up with a clear message that money and *things* equal love, and that those who have the most are loved the most.

Because on an emotional level these children still feel unsatisfied, they feel the need for more *things* to fill the void. Any time a request for some new *thing* is denied, the child must deduce that he or she is not worthy of it somehow, and, therefore, is not loved. If the reason for the denial is a financial one, the parent must then find a way to work and earn more to pacify the child, and the situation becomes a "catch 22" where the parent works more to fill the void, thereby creating a larger void due to his absence. The problem is self-perpetuating.

My experience has shown that children of working or absent mothers and fathers are often showered with gifts not only out of guilt but also as a means of bribing the child for the time the parent has been absent. In essence, the parent is saying, "See all the extra things you get to have because Mommy is not here with you during the day." Before long, these rewards carry over as incentives for the completion of ordinary chores and responsibilities that every young child and teen should be expected to do as a way of contributing to the family and preparing them for adulthood. Oftentimes, these rewards become the standard operating procedure for bribing the youngster into simply behaving appropriately.

How many times have you observed a frustrated parent's attempt to coax a child with treats or toys in exchange for good behavior? The child is now more motivated by material rewards than by any feeling of obligation or sense of right and wrong? He has learned his lesson well.

From a teacher's perspective, I have observed that these are the same children who balk at the idea of doing an assignment simply for practice and for which there is no grade to be earned. Furthermore, on occasions such as a child taking home a report card to be returned with a parent's signature, many of these children expect a reward of some kind for merely doing what was asked. They are clearly disappointed and feel cheated when none is offered. Doing "something for nothing" is a foreign concept to them, and those who do a task simply because it is expected of them are labeled as "fools" or "losers."

Not only has their sense of responsibility been corrupted, these children often have a diminished sense of charity and social obligation toward their fellow man. Just as they are unwilling to **do** something for nothing, they are also unwilling to **give** something for nothing. That is not to suggest that these attitudes are in any way limited to children of working mothers or that exceptional kids do not come from families where their mothers work outside the home. However, there is a mountain of evidence to support the general decline in the moral character of today's youth throughout the world. Better and more involved parenting could go a long way towards curing some of these ills.

With more parental involvement and supervision, perhaps television, movies, music, and video games with all of their violence, sexual situations, and vulgar language would not have the opportunity to affect our young people as profoundly as they have in recent years. The working mother who only has a few precious hours in the evening to shop for groceries, make dinner, do laundry and some light housework to ready herself and her family for the next workday will rarely interrupt a child who is quietly watching television or playing on the computer to have a conversation or read a book. This is not because she chooses to neglect him, but rather because his situation does not elicit the same sense of urgency that the others require in order to keep the household running smoothly. We seem to be more concerned that our children have clean clothes and clean homes than clean minds.

Today's youth are typically described as angry and without conscience. I believe that beneath every expression of anger lies a deep sadness that stems from some feeling of worthlessness or abandonment. These children are crying out for attention (even if it has to be negative attention) because their own parents either will not or cannot take the time to spend with them because of hectic schedules. Just as a crying baby draws the attention of every mother within earshot, we all feel the repercussions of those children whose parents have not spent the necessary time to make their children feel loved and needed. These are the children who gain this much-needed attention by either killing their parents, classmates, or more often than not, themselves.

These are also the kids who join gangs to experience a sense of family and acceptance, and once that line has been crossed, it becomes an issue of territory and loyalty and what extremes they will go to in order to demonstrate that loyalty. These acts, no matter how heinous and criminal, are worth it in the eyes of these children in order to gain a sense of belonging and the assurance that someone will step up and protect them should the need arise. They feel vulnerable and naked because their own families have left them without that emotional cloak of security. Just as the pedophile knows by instinct which child will go with him, gang members know which kids are more likely to join them, and with "safety and strength in numbers" as their motivator, they need all the members they can recruit.

Our country has been in an uproar as of late about the increased violence among our young people involving guns. We need to be reminded that guns have been a part of our society for literally hundreds of years, and it is the condition of the hearts and minds of our children that should be examined to determine what motivates them to choose guns to settle their disputes. You see, without the inclination to use it, a gun is nothing more than a tool. This is best demonstrated by the fact that in cities like Boston where strict gun laws have made it difficult for civilians to purchase or obtain guns, there has been a surge in the sale of knives on the street and an increase in stabbings and other knife-related crimes.

We as parents need to uncover the source of the anger and do our best to instill in our children a sense of the right and wrong way to resolve conflict. Anger is a natural and sometimes necessary emotion, but there is a healthy way to manage and control anger. This type of training must begin in the first years of life.

Many of the problems and insecurities that children develop as teens can oftentimes be alleviated or at least reduced in the earlier years if the child has a strong foundation of constant, nurturing parental interaction. Unfortunately, the parent who is gone from home the majority of the day is typically unable to provide this kind of attention on a consistent basis.

If you do not remember another line from this book, please remember this--**There is no material possession you can give your children**

that will ever mean more to them than the time you have spent together. There will be opportunities in the years they are in school to make a financial contribution to the family if you wish, and that will be the time when those material possessions start to affect the way a child sees himself through the eyes of his peers. When children are small, they need the comfort and reassurance that Mom and Dad are nearby to protect them and make them feel loved and secure.

It's hard to say
"I'll walk away"
And choose the job of mother.
But choose I will
For I know still
For me there is no other.

There's work begun
That is not done,
For you, my son,
I'll leave it.
There's much to do,
And all for you
I'll give for I believe it.

Chapter 3:
How to Cut the Umbilical Cord to Your Job

One of the questions that may be troubling you as you consider the prospect of putting your career on hold might be addressed in the following way: How do you give up your job without some sense of letting down the people you are working for or giving up the status you have achieved?

When I left teaching just before the birth of my first child, I had many mixed emotions. Seven of the ten years I had been teaching, I acted as head of the English department, a position of modest authority and respect. I also felt that I had made a significant contribution to changing the lives of the young people who had passed through my classroom over the years. Deep within I wondered who else would devote as much time and energy to the kids who really needed a responsible, caring adult in their lives?

The people I worked with and for had become like a second family to me. My principal was and still is one of my dearest friends. How could I let her down by quitting? After much introspection and prayer, I decided to take a leap of faith. After all, I had devoted ten years of my life to all these other people and their children. I could easily give half that to my own. Still, doubts would creep in like "What if this job or one comparable to it is not available to me when I am ready to return?"

Much to my relief/disappointment, the next school year came off without even one desperate phone call asking for my expertise or aid. I soon realized that the only area that had really suffered in my absence was my ego. What a blow! **I** had been replaced and soon realized that everyone really is expendable with few exceptions. Unless you are self-employed or the true visionary and original creator of your company such as Martha Stewart or Vera Wang, your job could probably be filled quite handily, whether you would like to admit it or not. The role of mother to your children, however, can only and should only be filled by one woman—YOU! Many mothers today choose to hire that job out and merely act in a supervisory or consulting capacity, but our children are as original and unique as Vera Wang's designs, and without her own hand to guide the design, she would be left with an imposter's frock on which to put her name.

I discovered after leaving my job that I could still keep up with my coworkers and friends and see them on the occasions of my choosing. These friendships outside of work have grown even stronger without the pressures of the job surrounding them.

If the work you have done is to your credit, perhaps the job will still be there for you should you decide to return, and you are certain to have a fresh, new perspective to offer. You may also decide after a year or so of reflecting on your old job that it was more drudgery and less fulfilling than you ever realized, and you would be better served to pursue other avenues of employment when the time is appropriate. Often when we are in the midst of employment, there is little time to take a long, hard look at the job we do because we are too busy trying to do it. You would be amazed at how many life-changing decisions have been made while folding a pile of laundry or nursing a hungry baby!

O child of mine,

Was there the time

To give you all you needed?

To hear your dreams

And give the means,

To fly with fears unheeded?

Chapter 4:
Avoiding the Pitfalls of Daycare

When a mother stays home to care for her child many benefits begin to emerge. The child has a greater sense of security knowing where and with whom he will be each day. I have known some mothers who have their children in so many different forms of daycare (i.e. mother's-day-out at church, taking the child to someone else's house, having someone come to the home, etc.) that the child is literally lost every morning wondering where he is destined to spend his day.

Children, who attend regular daycare, although it may seem to provide stability, are often subjected to the unpredictable behavior of the other children, as well as the staff, not to mention the possibility of contracting every disease and virus known to man.

Children are going to become sick occasionally. Nature uses these experiences as a way of developing their immune systems, but many children in daycare are exposed to viruses and germs on a much larger scale, and sometimes these illnesses are not just a case of the sniffles. We had an outbreak of meningitis in our area last year where several children died, and had my children been school age, I would not have hesitated to keep them home until the threat had passed. My husband and I even took turns going to church so that we could keep them from being exposed until the vaccination had the required two weeks to take effect. If I had been a working mother, I would have been forced to leave them in a potentially life-threatening situation each day or risk compromising my job to protect them.

Did you know that according to an article in the July 2002 issue of *Better Homes and Gardens,* "More babies die of SIDS (sudden infant death syndrome) in one year than all children who die of cancer, abuse, heart disease, pneumonia, AIDS, cystic fibrosis, and muscular dystrophy combined"? Furthermore, the article goes on to say, "A study in the journal *Pediatrics* found that a significant percentage of SIDS deaths occur in day-care settings. One possible reason: Children in day care are more likely to be put to sleep on their stomachs or to be found sleeping on their stomachs"—something that you as a mother with many fewer children to attend to could possibly monitor more diligently.

By keeping your children at home, you are minimizing their risks of illness, injury, and even death because you have reduced their chances of exposure and have eliminated the opportunity for poor supervision or poor judgment. In addition, should your child actually become sick, often in the middle of the night, he or she will never have to feel your sense of frustration in knowing you have to face a full day of work early the next morning or make arrangements to be out for the day. As a working mother, staying at home with a sick child may become a time your child relishes so much that he may decide to be "sick" more often just to have a day at home with you.

Another advantage to consider is: How much more likely are you as a parent to sit and read to your child? Almost all daycare workers are responsible for several children at one time. How could your child possibly receive the same one-on-one attention you could provide? Most reasonably priced daycare programs can only afford to offer lower fees by increasing the number of children enrolled.

As a parent, I can tell you of many times that I did not feel like doing what my child either needed or wanted from me, but I did it because I loved him as only a parent could. How could you possibly expect that kind of devotion from someone other than a parent, and your child deserves to have all his needs met whenever possible?

In our country, the average daycare worker earns less than we pay our parking attendants. While the salaries are among the lowest, the turnover rate is among the highest. Most adults burn out quickly when dealing with children on a daily basis, and while quality personnel are difficult to find, they are even harder to keep. How stable an environment could it possibly be for your child to have to adjust to a new stranger every few weeks? How would we as adults like having to adjust to a new supervisor as frequently?

Many working and non-working parents have transferred that need for a competitive edge found in the workplace to their child's education. They believe that the earlier they enroll their child in some form of daycare or preschool, the better advantage that child will have when kindergarten arrives. I was surprised and relieved to learn the contrary.

When my older son began kindergarten, the school he attended also offered a preschool program. Even though I am a firm believer in keeping children at home until they are required to attend school, I began to consider what many parents who choose daycare or preschool have come to believe, and I wondered if he might start off at a slight disadvantage in a class where many had already completed one full year of schooling.

Being a teacher myself, I wanted to know what skills he would need in order to begin the year successfully, and I would do my best to teach those over the summer. His teacher explained that she always begins the year with the number "one" and the letter "A" for all students. She further reassured me that in her fourteen years of teaching kindergarten, her best readers and those students who performed best on the standardized tests had consistently been those students who had been at home with their mothers and <u>not</u> those students who had attended daycare or preschool. She had no idea of the degree of importance I placed on her comments or how reaffirming they were for me.

For the single mother, daycare is certainly a necessary aspect of her life, but when it comes to the emotional, physical, and educational welfare of a child, being at home with his or her mother is and should be the optimum choice.

For the written word,

To go unheard,

Is to leave the mind unfed.

For the child in need,

Who begins to read,

Can feast on the unread.

Chapter 5:
Read to Succeed

Reading to your child at an early age almost guarantees that he or she will be more successful at reading when the time comes. When mothers read to their children, these children often begin reading earlier than those of mothers who did not. Speaking as an educator, your child's ability and interest in reading will more greatly impact his/her success in school than any other skill.

In the ten years I taught in public schools, I have seen the disturbing results of the breakdown in the family unit. More children are being medicated for behavioral problems than ever before, standardized tests continue to show decreases in performance, and students are still dropping out of school at an alarming rate. We are not breeding offspring who are inherently less intelligent and less able to behave themselves than we were at their ages; we are breeding a generation of individuals who are generally less nurtured than we were.

Often there is no one at home to read to children and help them with their homework; therefore, a love of reading and the ethic of doing well in school have typically not been instilled. When there is no one paying attention and policing children's schooling to make sure they are completing the requirements of their education, children often fail. When we fail as adults, it can certainly be a devastating experience, but most healthy, mature adults eventually manage to recover. When children fail, they often brand themselves as failures and sometimes lack the emotional skills to rise above these feelings.

Another reason many high school students today are graduating without the ability to read is that a vast majority are so visually stimulated from the unsupervised use of television, video games, and Internet access (often a working mother's saving grace when it comes to accomplishing her own work without distraction) that any other attempt to capture their attention seems mundane or boring. The idea of picking up a book purely to read for pleasure is rarely a consideration when the average adolescent is given a choice of how to spend his or her free time.

These children are a middle school teacher's nightmare. All but gone are the days of lessons taught in lecture form at the middle school level. Today's student is more often than not a visual learner with poor listening skills. We used to refer to it as "tap dancing naked" in order to capture their attention, and many successful middle school graduates struggle when reaching high school where the lecture mode is still alive and well.

I believe that this visual over-stimulation and some parents' inability to discipline their children effectively and consistently are responsible for much of the Attention-Deficit/Hyperactivity Disorder (ADHD) being diagnosed today. According to the *Diagnostic & Statistical Manual of Mental Disorders (fourth edition)*, which is the most widely used diagnostic criteria for ADHD, "Approximately 2-5% of the school age population in the USA has been diagnosed with one of the three types of ADHD. Strangely, ADHD is three to four times more likely to occur in males than females." Perhaps the fact that males in general are more visually stimulated than females accounts for this fact.

Students who do not excel in reading are almost always destined to become poor writers, poor spellers, and most importantly, poor communicators as adults. What parent would not want his or her child to have every possible advantage when it comes to education? We as parents are the original, as well as the most influential teachers of our children, so why not seize the opportunity to make a difference in your children's futures by reading to them when you have time to do it in a relaxed, unrushed atmosphere (the sort that working mothers often have difficulty creating)? Furthermore, hold them accountable for what was read by asking a few questions at the end of a reading session or story. This will create a habit of effective listening skills that will enrich every area of their education and, more importantly, their lives.

"Polite boys do."

"Of course, you may."

"You should always know to ask."

"We don't say that."

"Do what? No way!"

"Don't even bother to ask?"

Chapter 6:
The True Value of Your Time

How often have you witnessed someone disciplining a child and muttered under your breath that you would never behave or speak in such a way to a child of your own? Have you and your mother ever disagreed on the way to handle any situation? Have you identified in your adult life some mistakes made by one or both of your parents in raising you?

The reality is that no one, and that includes family members, will ever have exactly the same set of values and methods for handling your children as you. Even you and your spouse will find it challenging to agree in every instance on the best way to parent your children.

The first five years of your children's lives will be the most important in establishing what kind of individuals they will become. These are the years when they are the most easily influenced. After your children start school, they will be shaped by the influence of other adults and other children. If they do not have a firm foundation established by you, they will be left at the mercy of those who cross their paths.

Establishing a strong foundation takes time. If your child is in daycare eight, nine, or ten hours a day, and at home with you for the four hours or so before bedtime, who has more opportunity to interact with and influence your child? I know of a few working mothers whose babies have called their sitters "Mommy" first, instead of their own mothers. I have a relative who brags that her daughter loves her babysitter so much that the child cries hysterically each time she is forced to leave. This confusion is easy to understand. Even an infant knows that her mother naturally should be the one who spends the most time with her and provides her the most care.

I happen to be from the South where good manners are a solid requirement; therefore, good manners are high on my list of priorities for my children. Teaching your children to show respect and consideration for others must begin at birth, and it has been my experience that well-mannered children make a lasting first impression on the adults they encounter in life. Sometimes that first impression will dictate how a teacher views your child for the rest of the year. Good manners are simply good habits. Unfortunately, as more time passes, the less emphasis is placed on good manners, which makes those who possess them a rare find. If children are told "please," "thank you," "excuse me," "I'm sorry," etc. on a regular basis, they cannot help but adopt these phrases as part of their everyday dialog.

Many daycare providers have so many different children from so many different backgrounds that they might hesitate to influence the children they keep in any way for fear that they may be overstepping their bounds or that one uniform way of handling a situation may not be appropriate for all children concerned. What is important to the healthy development of your child may not be important at all to your childcare provider.

Working mothers often experience a certain amount of guilt about the time they spend away from their children, and therefore are reluctant to be strong disciplinarians during that limited time. How likely is it that you and your daycare provider will have exactly the same philosophies when it comes to disciplining your child? What kind of mixed signals will your child be receiving during the day when what is acceptable to your babysitter may be completely unacceptable to you and vice versa? During the course of an interview with a prospective childcare provider, to cover every conceivable situation that may arise in the care of your child would be impossible.

Family values and discipline strategies are personal decisions, and while you may question some of what you do with your own children, as any good parent does, hopefully you will not have to spend the rest of your life trying to undo bad habits taught by a stranger or relative, no matter how well-meaning.

The stranger of today,

Seems much stranger than before.

We hear of acts so horrid,

They grow harder to ignore.

But what of those,

Not strange to you,

With whom you've left your child?

Will they behave and think like you?

Watch as you would?

Do what you'd do?

With tempers meek and mild?

Chapter 7:
The Imperfect Stranger

How many times have we heard the tragic story of a child losing his or her life at the hands of a stranger? We have shed tears of anger and despair for the families of children who have been abducted and later found murdered or never found at all. This kind of tragedy is a parent's worst nightmare. It may be surprising to learn that according to Gavin de Becker, best-selling author and America's leading expert on predicting violent behavior, "Your child stands a better chance of [dying] from a heart attack than being abducted and murdered by a stranger." The adults whom the child knows actually pose the greatest threat.

Pedophiles come from every walk of life. They place themselves in positions where they are sure to come into contact with children. We often hear the stories of children who have been sexually abused by a teacher, coach, neighbor, or minister. As parents, we are horrified to think we have placed our child's safety and well being into the hands

41

of such a monster. When these acts happen to a child who is school age, we are outraged. Often it takes the courage of one child to tell what has been happening to him and possibly others, but what if it is happening to your infant or toddler who has not yet acquired the necessary language skills and is unable to tell you of these incidents? Speech is a God-given tool designed to aid us in survival. A crying infant or toddler may be diagnosed for every ailment from colic to teething. Rarely, if ever, would we think to add abuse to that list.

Can we as a nation ever forget the trial of Louise Woodward, the nanny accused of shaking little Matthew Ethan to death? She was later acquitted of these charges because the only witness to the event was Matthew himself, and he took that knowledge to his grave. How well do you really know the person with whom your child is left during the day or night? The fact that the popularity of devices such as the nanny cam (a camera easily concealed in a clock, radio, teddy bear, or other fixture of a room and is designed for secret surveillance) have grown exponentially in the last few years is some indication that even the best agencies in the daycare business have questionable employees.

The parents who have hired nannies or other in-home help are willing to spend the extra money to have someone come to their home to keep their child, so the child does not have to leave the comfort and security of familiar surroundings. However, that comfort and security also provide an opportunity for privacy that public daycare does not.

Even if you were to place a camera in every room of your home, which would in some instances be considered criminal, there is still the outside of the house to consider. Is your nanny permitted to leave the home while caring for your child, perhaps to go to the park, mall, or grocery store? No camera in the world could capture every event in the child's day except the one in your child's brain, and he or she may not be able to process fully what has been seen and heard, much less communicate it to you, as was true in Matthew's case. Even older children are often bribed, threatened, or convinced in other ways not to tell. Furthermore, all the technology available today will not prevent the violence from occurring; these devices will simply make you aware of the offense after the fact.

Not all tragedies occur at the hands of evildoers. Sometimes accidents occur while children are in the care of well-meaning caregivers. Certainly there are incidents which could not be prevented no matter who is in charge of your child, but what about the ones that are purely an error in judgment? Whether it be a neighborhood teen or a trusted friend or family member, different people have different ideas about what is safe and what is sensible.

Take for instance the mother who despite her own feelings of uneasiness reluctantly made the decision to place her baby in daycare. She did all she knew to do to find a competent, licensed daycare provider and finally settled on a woman who came highly recommended by someone from the mother's church. The mother came to the woman's residence to inspect the premises and to leave her infant for an hour or so as a trial visit in order to see how the infant and the provider would react to one another. When she arrived, she made a mental note that there were only two other children there, and the facility seemed to be adequate and conducive to the professional and personal care of small children, so she decided to leave her baby for the agreed upon stay.

After a period of just under two hours, the mother could stand the separation no longer and returned to pick up her son. She noticed that it took an unusually long time for the daycare provider to answer the door, but when the woman finally came to the door, she assured the mother that all was well and that the baby had been napping. When the mother went to retrieve her baby, she noticed that the baby had been placed on his stomach to nap on top of a cushiony mattress and blanket. The baby had suffocated.

After the police arrived, they discovered that a total of thirteen children were actually present in the house, hence the delay in answering the door. The provider lost her license, while the mother lost her only son, hardly an even trade by anyone's standards.

Another story I will never forget is that of William and Michelle Puckett whose babysitter left their 11-month-old son in a locked car on a hot, steamy day while she went into the mall for a few minutes that turned out to be two-and-a-half hours. The baby was later found by a police officer, but died within a few hours at a local hospital from exposure to the heat. There was no malicious intent on the part of the sitter, as proven by the fact that she left her own baby in the car as well. Fortunately, her child was a few months older and was able to withstand the heat with few side effects.

Unfortunately, that same child will be an adult by the time his mother is released from prison. Even good parents do not have all the answers, but if your child lost his life or were critically injured while in the care of another, how could you ever really convince yourself that more could not have been done or that the whole incident could not have been avoided if you had only been there?

Even the best parents deserve a break every now and then. We should not be motivated by fear, but we must understand the risks involved when we leave our flesh and blood in the care of others. Choose carefully with whom you will trust your child's life, and if you believe in prayer, pray!

Stop saving for a rainy day,

Start saving for a baby day.

The rain could come at any time,

But babies come in months of nine.

So make a plan that you can do,

Before you're three instead of two.

A little sacrifice today,

Will ease your mind on baby day.

Chapter 8:
Plan for Your Income Adjustment

Surviving on one income while you are staying at home with your children is very feasible. Planning is the key.

In this day of birth control and technological advances in medicine, we are afforded a luxury that many of our own mothers did not have. In most cases, we are able to choose when we want to start a family. Because we have this choice, we should also be able to plan financially for that event. You should not wait until the baby arrives to make the adjustment to one income. Granted, there are some cases where the main breadwinner does not bring home enough to support the family entirely, but everyone's idea of "enough" is relative.

When my husband and I were first married, we decided almost right away that when the time came for us to start a family, I would stay at home with our children at least until they were school age. In order to accomplish that, we would have to make the most of our two salaries while we were both still drawing a paycheck. We elected to reduce our expenses and live only on my salary, while putting his into savings each month. Through the course of the first year of our marriage and the following nine months of my pregnancy, we saved enough money to reduce our debt significantly, while still managing to build our savings. If we had wanted, we could have delayed having a family even longer, which would have put us in even better shape.

When I quit teaching to be a full-time mother, my husband continued with his teaching position. Certainly, we can all agree that teachers earn pretty meager salaries, comparatively speaking, so the odds of your being successful are pretty strong. Small modifications in your style of living can add up to huge savings. If you are already living paycheck-to-paycheck with two salaries, maybe it is time to consider ways to reduce your monthly debt.

If you live in a large home with a sizeable mortgage, perhaps you could consider moving into a smaller home just until you are back at work. However, if this is the home of your dreams and you could not bear to sell it, try cutting down on your extra expenses such as eating out (including lunches), going to movies instead of renting an occasional one, spending more than is really necessary on gifts for friends and family, etc. Set a limit for birthday and Christmas gifts (depending on the age and relationship of the recipient).

Limit yourselves to one dinner out per week with few exceptions, and take your lunch to work. Chances are what you pack for yourself will be more nutritious and certainly less expensive than what you would buy otherwise. Use the extra time you save not sitting in a restaurant with long lines and lousy service to run a few errands, read a really great book, or take that ever popular "power nap" you have been hearing so much about lately.

You should become proficient at cooking at home anyway because your children will want to eat **at least** three meals a day, and it is not feasible to suggest takeout for every one. With the money you are saving each month, you could possibly double up on your house note or put your money into an account or investment that could earn you interest.

Pay off your car notes, if possible, and make sure the vehicle you are driving will accommodate your growing family comfortably for a few years because a new vehicle is probably out of the question for a while. Pay your insurance premiums for the whole year if you can to avoid service charges for monthly or quarterly payments.

Speaking of service charges, what about your bank accounts? Many banks these days offer free checking. Often it is just a matter of direct depositing your paycheck, which saves you time and money as well. Keep your ATM card for emergencies only, or cut it up and throw it away. Never use a service that charges you a fee to access your own money. Have you noticed how many full service banks there are right inside most grocery stores? Why not save yourself an extra trip by banking somewhere that you already go every week anyway? Many of these banks are open twenty-four hours a day, seven days a week just like the stores that house them. How much more convenience could you possibly need?

Before you make a trip to the grocery store, do your homework. Always make a list to prevent unnecessary return trips, and avoid the displays near the checkout lines that are designed to encourage impulse buying. One of the most effective ways to save money is by clipping coupons and paying special attention to the sale papers that come in the mail. Many grocery and discount stores will honor other stores' coupons and will match their weekly sales, which saves you the trouble and expense of traveling from store to store. This can save you hundreds if not thousands of dollars per year with minimal effort on your part.

The main goal is to reduce your existing debt by a significant margin or eliminate it altogether and/or to save money to accommodate your upcoming debt should you need to upgrade your living conditions after your children are born. If you make these practices a part of your everyday life, you will be amazed at how much money you can save, and if you are like me, you may even experience a certain amount of guilt for not having started sooner.

Having another mouth to feed will certainly add to your expenses, and when food goes in, it has to come out, so diapers will be a considerable expense as well. Breastfeeding is not only the best way to nourish your baby, but it is a natural way to save money too. According to the latest research by the National Institute of Child Health and Human Development, breastfeeding has also been shown to increase the intelligence scores of infants born prematurely and those born full-term of normal weight. Recent studies also show that babies who died of SIDS were less likely to have been breast-fed.

In order for your child to reap the full benefits of breastfeeding, you must be committed to several months of total accessibility, which is one practice you can adopt much more easily if you are at home all day. I have heard too many horror stories of mothers pumping their breasts or actually breastfeeding their babies while driving to work. I shudder to think what the headlines would read if an accident were to occur.

You might also be surprised at how much it actually costs you to work outside the home. Expenses such as dry cleaning; gas, tolls, and parking for your automobile; fares for other forms of transportation;

makeup; perfume; hair care products; business suits or other career apparel; pantyhose; dress shoes; lunches, as well as take-out for dinners that you might have prepared yourself if you had been home; travel expenses incurred but not covered by your employer; and most importantly, DAYCARE to name a few, are all reduced, if not eliminated, by your staying home. You can also save money on automobile insurance if your vehicle is no longer driven daily for commuting to work because it is then considered a luxury vehicle.

Many couples have little idea what they really spend each month, but identifying the areas where money could be saved might be easier than you think. Consolidate your debt into one credit card, and keep that one alone for use every month. Make sure it is a card that charges no annual fee EVER. Each of you should have a copy of the credit card to use. My husband puts all his expenses on the credit card, whether it be gas, dry cleaning, some home improvement need, etc. I also charge my groceries and any other purchases on the credit card. Paying off those balances each month is sometimes painful, but absolutely essential to progress.

Both my husband and I pay ourselves a small allowance twice a month. After all, I deserve some reward for the work I do at home. Any purchases that are purely considered luxury expenses, such as new decorative pieces for the home, clothes that are not work-related, shooting a round of skeet at the gun club, buying bait for a fishing trip with a buddy, or any other item or activity that clearly should not come from the household budget must be saved for and paid for out of our allowances. This method really cuts down on impulse buying and forces us to evaluate every purchase carefully for its affordability as well as desirability.

There should be <u>one</u> designated bill payer in the family, and that person should keep the only checkbook. The checkbook should be balanced continuously. This will prevent any confusion in the actual amount of funds available and keep you from incurring any returned check and insufficient funds charges. Our checks are used solely for paying bills and the occasional expense where a credit card is not accepted or for charitable contributions; therefore, we rarely have to pay to reorder checks. Banking online is another way to avoid reordering checks and having to pay for postage. It also alleviates the guesswork of when a payment will arrive, which in turn could prevent a late charge or finance charge. Some credit cards will raise your interest rate after only one late payment. In addition, try to take advantage of those accounts that automatically charge to your credit card each month.

By using our monthly credit card and bank statements for reference, there is no question at the end of each month as to where our money was spent. If you have more money going out each month than you have coming in, this period of adjustment is already overdue, and having children at this time would probably not be a wise decision. When children are added to a marriage, the results can be exhilarating, exhausting, and at times, trying. Add to that the burden of financial difficulties, and you create a mix that can become extremely volatile, as well as toxic to a marriage.

More than two years may be required to achieve the financial goal that will allow for one of you to stay at home, but with a few sacrifices, it can be done. Make sure that the decisions you make are truly based on what is best for your children and not what you believe **you** need to feel successful. Small children have no concept of the square footage or value of a home. They just know that if home is where their family is, it will always be the best place to live.

I've put the pen to paper,

And it really cannot work.

How can I add some income

Without feeling like a jerk?

If home is where my heart is,

Then home is where I'll stay.

Proof positive "Where there's a will,

There has to be a way."

Chapter 9:
O.K., So You Still Have to Work

If giving up a second income is absolutely impossible for you to do after every solution has been considered, why not find a job that you could do from home? According to the *Gale Encyclopedia of Childhood and Adolescence*, "In the early 1990's, home-based businesses started by women were the fastest-growing type of business. The number of women employed in these ventures tripled between 1985 and 1991."

We as a country are now in full swing in our technological growth where working at home has become a popular feasible option. There are many jobs available to stay-at-home moms who are in need of additional income. These jobs are geared toward mothers in particular and are designed to allow you to put your family first. There are even websites and books such as, *101 Best Home-Based Businesses for Women* by Priscilla Y. Huff available to help you identify ways to earn money at home.

Some at-home occupations require a minimal amount of training, which can also be completed at home through correspondence for a nominal fee. Some of these in the medical field such as medical transcription and medical billing can be quite lucrative because you are paid an hourly rate. You have the flexibility to work as much or as little as you like.

There are even some at-home jobs that require no special training at all. If you can stuff envelopes or assemble the parts for a simple gadget, you can earn extra money from your home. These options may be worth considering even after your children reach school age.

How wonderful would it be to have the freedom to attend your children's school programs, conferences, parties, field trips, and other special events designed to involve parents? What if your child becomes sick in the middle of the night and must stay home from school for a day? What do you do with a child who has summers off and holidays different from those your employer observes? If you are working outside the home, what do you do with your child between the time he or she is out of school and you are home from work? These are all questions that plague the working mother.

Many people are choosing to resume their fulltime jobs from home by telecommuting whenever possible, with the cooperation of their employers. All that is needed is a P.C. with a modem and Internet access and a fax machine. (At the end of your first year at home, you can write these purchases off as business expenses, along with a portion of mortgage related to your home office, Internet provider fees, etc.)

The benefits of telecommuting to the employee are fairly obvious, but what may not be so obvious are the benefits to the employer. In a recent article in the April 2000 issue of *Working Mother* magazine it was revealed that an employer who allows an employee to work from home could save as much as $10,000 per year in expenses. "A recent survey by the International Telework Association and Council found that a satisfied employee is less likely to leave the company, lowering turnover costs and saving about $8,000. Plus, missing work for a sick child or parent isn't a problem when your office is in the spare bedroom, leading to less absenteeism and potential savings of $2,000."

The article goes on to explain that by allowing you to telecommute, your employer may also be eligible for a tax credit. "A new federal law grants tax credits to companies in five congested cities (Chicago, Houston, Los Angeles, Philadelphia, and Washington, D.C.) if they allow employees to work from home. Why? Fewer commuters [mean] less pollution—and traffic—[and] overcrowded roads."

Working from home fulltime does require some in-home daycare, but often just knowing you are in the house is enough to ease your mind as well as your child's and to make a difference in both of your days. In essence, you experience the best of both worlds, thereby creating a winning situation for you, your child, and your employer.

Just one more minute,
One more day,
To hold you in it,
I would pray.

Just one more chance,
To say the words,
I should've said,
That went unheard.

But that is not to be, I fear,
And I am left with just a tear,
And memories of days gone past,
I never knew they'd go so fast,
Or stop so short,
And would not last.

We live our lives,
And take for granted,
The seeds for our tomorrows planted,
But some tomorrows never come,
You or your loved one taken from,
The ones whose cries are heard to say,
"Just one more minute,
One more day."

Chapter 10:
Life Holds No Guarantees

September 11, 2001 was quite a day of reckoning for us all! All the mothers and fathers who perished in the Twin Towers that morning took for granted that they would return home to their children that same evening, but because of the violent acts that transpired that day, it was not to be. What better example of the uncertainty of tomorrow do we as a nation need?

We are surrounded every day with the news of the tragic death of a young child or parent. The horrors that took place at Columbine High School opened our eyes once again to the brevity of life, as did the bonfire tragedy at Texas A&M University. There are airline disasters almost every month as of late, and deaths due to breast cancer and other illnesses have taken a huge toll on the mothers, daughters, sisters, and friends in our lives. We often take it for granted that we will endure for the normal life expectancy, that the natural order will prevail, and that our children will outlive us, but what if God has a different plan? We have no way of knowing when our time or those of our children will come.

If the unthinkable were to happen and your child lost his or her life either through illness, accident, or an act of violence, wouldn't you feel an even greater sense of grief and regret in knowing you did not spend every possible moment with your child when you had the opportunity?

What if you were the one whose life were cut short by illness or ended accidentally or at the hands of another? If your children were still young, would you have wished for the opportunity to pour into them as much of your guidance, wisdom, and influence as possible to ensure them the greatest chance of becoming the healthy, productive adults you hoped them to be or at least give them as many of the tools they would need to cope in your absence?

In every case, the survivors of these tragedies have but one wish--to have had more time with the loved ones they have lost. Why cheat yourself or your children out of that time unnecessarily?

We have often heard the saying, "Live each day as if it were your last." If this truly were your last day on earth, is there any doubt that you would want to spend it with your children, and they with you?

Conclusion:

A wise person once observed that "What is popular is not always right, and what is right is not always popular." Staying at home with your children during their formative years is certainly not as popular an idea as it once was, but it is most assuredly the right one. All I ask is that you search your heart and make a decision that you know is the right one for you and your children. You will never have a second chance to spend their childhoods with them. Five years is not really too much to ask when you weigh the long-term benefits to you and your family. Many of you were willing to commit four or five years of your life to a university to help secure your future. You are willing to commit the same amount of time to paying off an automobile that you will ultimately trade for another. Why should the futures of your children be of any less value to you?

If you are not willing to invest the necessary time to provide your children with a strong sense of family, you can expect them to look for it elsewhere. Perhaps a gang might provide that sense of security and belonging, and those members rarely leave other members behind to fulfill employment obligations. There will be time to continue or begin your career after your children are in school. Being a stay-at-home mom is the gift of a lifetime, the one you give yourself and the one you give your children.